Roselle Angwin is a Cornish poet, author and painter whose work has won a number of awards. She read Anglo-Saxon, Norse and Celtic and followed that with a training in transpersonal psychology. Her work is influenced by these things, as well as by Zen and druidry.

Under the *Fire in the Head* banner she leads an international holistic creative writing programme ranging from the ecobardic 'Ground of Being' outdoor workshops, through intensive poetry, to novel-writing based on the psychology of myth.

As a poet, she has been involved in a number of interdisciplinary and often land-based arts projects, collaborating with other writers, and with artists, musicians, dancers and sculptors. Her poetry has been displayed on buses and cathedral websites, has appeared in numerous anthologies, been etched into glass, hung from trees, printed on T-shirts, carved into stone, metal and wood, painted, sung, composed to, choreographed, danced, performed—and eaten by sheep. Her novel, *Imago*, appeared in 2011.

Also by Roselle Angwin

Poetry
A Hawk into Everywhere *(with Rupert M. Loydell)*
Looking for Icarus
Hestercombe *(prints and poems, artist's book with Penny Grist)*
River Suite (*with Vikky Minette*)

Fiction
Imago

Non-fiction
Riding the Dragon — Myth and the Inner Journey
Creative Novel Writing
Writing The Bright Moment

As editor
Moor Poets 1
Confluence—anthology of work from the Two Rivers group

Bardo

Roselle Angwin

Shearsman Books

First published in the United Kingdom in 2011 by
Shearsman Books
58 Velwell Road
Exeter EX4 4LD

http://www.shearsman.com/

ISBN 978-1-84861-163-4

Acknowledgements
Grateful acknowledgment is made to the editors of the books or
journals in which some of the poems in this book first appeared:

'One True Thing' (earlier version) in *Soul Feathers* anthology (IDP,
for Macmillan cancer relief); 'What-are-the-birds-doing-with-the-
December-sky rap' in *Confluence* anthology (Root Creations/Two
Rivers); 'In the time of no time' in *Contemporary Haibun Online*;
'Summer Solstice, Merrivale' in *Soul of the Earth* anthology (Awen);
'The white noise of the universe' (earlier version) in
Looking For Icarus (bluechrome).

Contents

'[T]he essence of bardo . . . can . . . be applied to every moment of existence. The present moment, the now, is a continual bardo, always suspended between the past and the future.'

—*Francesca Fremantle*

if you take away the sum
of the manifest universe
what remains is light

One true thing

The land streams past the window. The heart asks for both clarity and paradox, aches equally for freedom and for joining, being part of and apart.

To be like a tree. To be that horse dreaming, one hoof delicately pointed, muzzle lowered and relaxed, at home completely in the day.

Tell me the truest thing you can, is what this journey seems to say.

Ridgeway *Near Uffington*

It was a hard ascent up to the chalklands into places that didn't know water. Then stepping into a sky bigger than anything except mind, and how we live sometimes as if the sky were not big enough to swallow us whole, holy, but that day we parted the tranches of barley like waves in a field canted towards the horizon and knew that we could fly, upwards into the scudding blue intervals; and later though you were a foot away I could hear your heartbeat through the chalk and the day breathing the greengold barley and the silvermauve grasses and little downland flowers that knew something of blue and the skylark kiting its song, and below us the white horse dreaming in its long slow sleep as it has for millennia and the sky came down anyway—a moment when we might enter someone else's life, and remember.

Ridgeway *Near Wayland's Smithy*

There are more layers than we can know or imagine, and here are some: sky gathering; emerald hills pressing upwards; and everything lit from within by this morning's hazy but irrepressible sunrise.

Here the stillness is alive: ancient and loud in its 5000-year-old silence.

All of life is contained in a hand, releasing a bird that we cannot see into the path of the wind that is not yet here; or perhaps has already passed.

Ridgeway *Scutchamer Knob*

On the horizon chrome-yellow light and light the colour of rust, water-gathering; and above, a pooling of night—of purple, ox-blood, indigo.

The tree is one with horizon and night. Holds still.

Ridgeway *Segsbury Camp*

Pleats of dawn light. Then sheets of noon. Then dusk.
Millennia &c.

This June solstice.

What you can't see from here is the beginning, or the end, of the
track that crosses your line of sight, though it's both invitation
and boundary. Beyond the earthworks the ridged hillside is a
pelt of the blood of history.

What you can't see from here are the figures in their helmeted
jerkined twos and threes, ragged and muddied; a gathering of
vapour, condensation on a membrane that remains invisible

just beyond our frequency, cohering from wind or drizzle, the
mist that might descend at the end of a moist summer day, a
flicker across the retina barely registered
          like the breeze through this sea of grasses, a quickening
of neurons

though you might just think the wind brings the clash of spear
and sword,
shouts and howls from mouths long stopped

          and maybe now at last, later, centuries, perhaps
          the laughter

that pares the darkness away from bone clean
as peeling an ash-wand.

Ridgeway *Barbury Castle*

Bliss of a simple mug of tea, respite from backpacks. A robin takes crumbs from my hand. In the perspex canteen window a photo of a green-barley crop circle, intricate and impenetrable. Is that a new one? I ask the girl. Yes, she says, I'll show you the article. Like a proud father her bloke hands me the paper. I found it, he says. Couple weeks ago. Coming and going all night on the hill, me and the boys, and never saw a thing. Next morning there it was.

A perfect pictorial representation of Pi, says the consulted astrophysicist, complete with decimal point and ellipsis for the recurring digits. The most complicated yet. Human-made, extra-terrestrial, geomantic, meteorological, fissure-energy, ephemeral echoes of megaliths? Connection between Pi and the Fibonacci sequence? Origins?

Explanations, you say, don't ever answer the bigger question: why?

Ridgeway *Hackpen Hill*

Later, in a perfect beech copse, round as a planet, we sit against trunks at the northern edge of Hackpen Hill, and look out over a 6-swirl fractal crop circle; simple and elegant. We don't talk.

Ridgeway *West Kennett Longbarrow*

Beetle. Drab daytime glow-worm. Barley-running day. Swifts.
Ploughing the skyline. Remember the city: vast loneliness; birds
willow water wide sky &c the only.

Then places that don't know water. The sussuration of time.
Arrow. Helios. Colours of the winds. Me—one interface of time
and space. Now.

The aching tree. You. Here. Waiting. Expectant. And un-.

Ridgeway

In the garden, at a meeting, on the road—my mind homes back to this place, reclines in its halls of grasses, backstrokes in its pools of silence.

The long men who stride these hills; their chalk horses.

Courtyard

1

Watching you from the window when you don't know I'm looking—sky falling slant through this span of glass, frost on the hillside and a few yellow spears still clinging to the willow for the warblers, paper-white narcissi at the fulcrum of waiting and becoming, and your purposeful stride, breath making visible atoms of air to halo, cobwebs stringing drops like tiny planets and the stream in the valley, my body still pliant and not quite separate yet (an articulation of grace), and you stop, and I know you'll be looking at the shooting winter garlic and all the time I'm here snug in the kitchen watching and thinking that one degree colder or one degree warmer we wouldn't be here at all, and how 'miracle' doesn't approach it.

2

Sometimes one's life is an open mouth asking question after question knowing there may be no answer.

Today after the difficult meeting I went with you out into the courtyard—together we bent to the paper-white narcissi, their brief scented faces lifted to the short grey day

and I longed to be opened again by sun, or moonlight, by rain— reminded how whole it all is, how perfect, even in its sometimes unending-seeming brokenness.

So much rain, drenching the willow, sliding off the roof, saturating the vegetable patch, but all the time I know it's on the inside.

3

Six o'clock again but in the evening this time, and we're here
again side-by-side on the wicker sofa with the terracotta pillows
like overstuffed thoughts

> and the rain; and we're listening to that, and to the
> silence that is the white noise of too many words
> unspoken. If I were to ask you what you are not saying
> you would say *by definition, nothing*

but I hear it all banging at the window, blind and flightless. Here
we are again, rain prickling the courtyard, the voice of the owl, a
full moon rising through bandages of cloud, and dark rolling in
like a drunk, like all that unknowing between what we are and
what we sense that we might be, if only

4

Fog unrolls from the river, ghosts up the valley so that the trees
stand behind themselves, lose a dimension.

Now the house is eclipsed, and we lose definition, belong to each
other again.

On this shortest day the fog steals the last of the light that we
were allowed, wraps us instead in white.

Rain

Even this late it happens: the twelve-bars from somewhere below on an old tin piano, the riff twisting in and out of storm, the blustery blues and the hooves of Herne's midnight horses measuring the salt-licked alley between us / and ourselves.

Somewhere else someone is dying, no I mean now, *now*—not just as in we all are, always, from birth on . . .

People come into your life, she said, for a reason, a season, and I expected her to continue 'or a lifetime', because I know this; but what she said was 'for a shag' (and I am wrong-footed, as I have been all year, which makes me think of you)

> — and I am not wanting to write about you, or any of this, but more about the wind hurling handfuls of stars out of some indigo bottomless pit against my window.

What I would like, he said, his frame jolting with Parkinsons and his voice shaking, is just one more time to feel the wind in my hair and me crouching on skis to launch myself from the top and keep on flying.

Even the house is juddering and the rain might never stop. The dog scratches at the door. Is it me who's howling?

Some mornings the best I might hope for is one more lemon dawn unfolding at the sea's horizon, and me with the eyes still to see it.

From the road you can barely see it, there in the trees, its green wood walls and ancient thatch true as winter wheat in moorland soil, a waymarker for walkers, fox and woodpecker, the lane narrow and rocky, steep and curved.

Descend the steps to the green door and open it
> onto light, as if you could walk right through to those southern hills. Place your foot over the threshold and— go on—lift the great key to the grandfather clock and start it. Jolt its heart.

Then take the chopper and that dry log and split the Yule kindling. Spell midwinter. The ring on the hearthstone will waken the house. Begin it. Call your name to the corners, to all the directions. Waken the ones who lived here before. Shout it out.

Open windows and doors for the smoke and put a match to the wood. Then press your ear to the inner skin of the timber walls. Can you hear it, that thrum, distant hum, like the sea in a shell? The swarm that blessed the house?

Are they still here, then, those bees with their promise of summer, and honey, and the drowsing of flowers, and love, bare-skinned and languid in the garden, beneath the thatched eaves, under trees? The promise of summer, and love?

The green water that is not air

Last night in the depths where the iris flowers wait out the winter in their bundle of roots the blue horse came and breathed at my neck. Was it I who was lying with the roots in the silt of the pool?

My father was the best-ever diver, and I was so proud when he climbed the cliffs higher than anyone, feet and feet above the sea, and shaped a pointed crescent and fell out falling into the air.

This summer I dreamed a naked woman cradling a salmon too big to fit into the bag at the airport. In J's dream he woke me from my fishy one by calling out: *the little stream is well cared-for . . .* Next morning in the hot gorge J and I stopped at the ruined monastery at Marsiac, and there was my woman and fish engraved in limestone, right beside the river.

Yes, it is me in the mud of the pool with the salmon and the iris, and on the cliffs high, too high, above me my father is still falling, falling through the green water that is not air.

Incident

Here of course you know it's not just about the knock on the door and it isn't actually like that, ever, but more to do with the terror that fills all available space in the silence
  after the firing. You can't start to name the dread.

Of course we're used to death, to naming the dead. But his hand to her still-warm face, her face that barely filled his hand—that place we can't start to know that he'll now inhabit forever.
  That now she has no name.
  That there is no heart pumping anywhere that she will hear again.
  That he can't believe this.

  That the moon

will go on rising, and the lights in the tower still lit, in that dread-filled silence.

Shall I go on? We were waiting for rain. Instead the din from the camp drummed our hearts, broke us all open, again. Again the ground will be watered with blood, and it's only bloodflowers can bloom here, in the dust, now.

everything there is

I can make you words from mud and rain, from bones and the
ache in the blood

words are an easy currency—their shiny sides tessellate neatly on
my tongue

but this is not a poem

if it's a poem you want better to ask the four winds, or get down
on your knees on damp earth in ashes and entrails

flailing, your own heart piercing your ribcage like a bird of prey

see the way a poem pushes its head even through tarmac, roots
cracking stone; lurks in unlit bus shelters with the stench of piss,
the fallout from five-in-the-morning doorways and broken glass

or ask autumn: shedding shoes and clothes and wading out
ankle-deep in leaf-fall beneath the sweet chestnuts

with everything there is wild and tender pulsing at the soles of
your bare feet

Someone needs to sing over the bones

Huddled at the foot of a vast mountain caught between plain and sky in the moon's bone-white slipstream a collection of runes and bones inhabiting a space that might spell

horse. Today I dwell in that space.

We are made and we cry to be made.

I remember the journey back from the islands west through the snowy mountains, travelling in our bliss, just at the moment when someone in the mountains was dying, and we did not feel his pain—or *was* it there, haunting with a vast loneliness that minute gap where we all stopped talking, the hiatus between the raising of the cup and the drinking, before the train resumed its motion, carrying us away?

Tamar

His voice, vortex of water, sun dropping; lights that turn,
hesitate, turn again
in the cold slick of stars.

November river a slow-breathing animal pied with avocet.

Sky a decoction of bleed colours shingling the water; orange
cartwheels of light
from the far bank. Actuality. Illusion.

Crossing the water

In the night the water swells, and we reach her house by boat.
On the shore, by the hedge, I hear the jaws of horses working,
eating up the darkness, making blue.

Small rain on leaves; the kind that scatters thought, and
regroups the scattered heart. No; but birdsong—a thousand
voices chattering in rain-time, spilling out of the goblet of the
valley.

The lit candles pale.

> She says my name over and over
> Though she does not know who I am.

Planting garlic at the winter solstice

The earth is crammed with invisible gods, their voices breaking out here now, at the nadir; we will need all the weight they can bring to turn back towards the sun. On the track a single blackthorn blossom raises its too-early pentangle to grey winter.

They have opened up the wells. I shall clean them. In my dream he has many faces; as I age he gets younger and younger. Black nights give way to gorse-filled days and then slowly the dark draws in again. The tide brings treasure to our feet and the old ways thrive unseen. Shadows play over us. I wake, and he is gone.

We light the candles, prepare the solstice feast. Her house is many shades of red, ochre, burnt earth. She has taken her place now; the earth is all womb and sun-standstill.

I move towards the tenebris.

We lift the solstice red to our lips, remember what has gone and what still needs to go. We are all stretched on the altar.

In the darkness, underground, the bulbs swell and something other is breathing.

Boleigh Fogou at midwinter 1

I am the dream of leaves in the bulb. I am the silence of under.
Am winter.

Stone I have known; the tender touch of brow under me; rain—
I am waiting for rain; rain and the eyebeams of the new young
sun.

I have softened into earth. I am in the blue dark, crouching. I
pray.

Midwinter at Boleigh Fogou 2

Light that turns, hesitates, reverses. Time's thumbprint marking
        my edge.
The dark pool of bitter midwinter—we're standing in
        underground water.

I am a bowl of silence. Rooks knock at my chest, beaking the
        leaf-winged air.
In the cove below light slides and breaks, and breaks.

Initiations of the present moment.

To give up one's life to depth. Nothing matters more than this
        everything.

Slipstream

This is sootfall, and a freefall too down from inky space, a wash of prussian and ochre, the swift hours' handprints visible and then gone.

You are a flush of light. You are night and the days piling up behind, a wake of ashes and stars.

You are a slow flow and tumble; you are the raven's call, and the deep bassoon thrum of the dark's waterfall, the staircase between worlds.

A flurry of embers. A smudge on the cool air. Fingerprint in space. The human race speeding up. Slipstream. Your own heart thrust into blossom.

Navigating memory

How one can never be truly prepared. Thinking about the gnostics' belief that we are all starfire falling into matter from the geometry of the singing spheres and outside the woodpeckers whose visits have been the most regular and constant thing this spring—watching their swinging foray and their swooping dipping flight and thinking again that really what counts is only how we do this trip here—this transient momentous fledging towards the sun and our certainty of further galaxies

and navigating memory the colour of distance which is the colour of moon-on-water, that which gradually develops from the negative—silver-gelatine or do I mean silver-nitrate—until we see the true form which is electromagnetic energy, and what matters is our continued trajectory, our Global Positioning devices tuned only to light

sky sutra
('mind is clear light' —Dalai Lama)

mist followed me up from the river but always ahead of me the
sky gleamed sapphire and I thought of how it was when I flew
into winter Geneva, skimming the mountains and lurching
through thick dank cloud, stepping out into sleet and knowing
all the time that just a few hundred feet above was pristine blue,
sunset chinking prisms off every cloud snow-peak, a milk of
cloud-lakes silking the flanks of real mountains and a whole
nation of rainbows

                a kind of private lightshow for the hell of it
that those below us couldn't see and that made everyone on that
plane gasp—for disbelief and amazement and joy not fear of
turbulence and the proximity of rock—as we plunged bucking
through that fog-blanket into such a different world

and how easy it is to forget

rain sutra

poetry again after such an absence, the house quiet, looking out at the courtyard, its many leaves fat with gratefulness for this spring, for rain, a bullfinch swaying like a tropical blossom on the pot choked with seeding cranesbill, one thrush, a late swallow checking out the eaves, rain making the woods more distant and impenetrable, its tap on the stone step an invitation

the valley's hush

rain settling in like conversation between lifelong friends; rain, plants, stone, birds at ease with themselves and each other, at ease with how the world needs to be

leaf sutra

how many years did it take, how much rain
and bone and sun, how much loss composted
into black peat to make this leaf, just this one
new leaf flickering green in the January ditch?

air sutra

the particles in these atoms
spell out buzzard
the rest
is wind and sky

water sutra

just a slight thickening
of the molecules that
make up water

the seal
is almost more wave
than matter

landscape sutra

bee, an inch from my iris
regarding me with its plural eyes

waterlily, poised on the threshold
of becoming

fritillary, gracing the shoulder
of the stone Buddha

nasal bone-whistle of the buzzard
planing its feathers like a stray idea
against cloud

cumulus, no more insubstantial
just because I know it to be so
my self, mere thought flicked away
in a flash like the fly
on the flanks of the grazing horse
picked out in the splinter
of lime-yellow light before
it falls and fades

September retreat sutra

Light rain, grass still warm underfoot. Cloud balances on Meldon's flanks. Spindle flowers and waterlily closed tight—already the birch is yellowing.

Elsewhere, scientists challenge the fabric of the cosmos.

Here we measure our own black holes against the broad sky, winkling them out of the cracks: the delusions and evasions of the ego, its fears, its doubts, its habits.

The rowan tree doesn't judge the wind; the robin eats out of my hand.

megalith sutra

clouds play the standing stones
in swift key-changes

stone row points the way—
stone circle says nowhere to go
but here

dog sutra

sky is a permanent question

gods come in thunder and lightning

every trail has two possible endings

anyone you meet is a friend until proven otherwise

nonetheless, do not trust where you land up until you've seen a winter, met those who consider it theirs

on the path a stray, your alter ego, follows you home under the stars

wolf sutra

even in this wastelot of a pen, this wolf is a poem: all claw and sinew; at rest, utterly relaxed; otherwise alert and muscular, ready to leap and spring; lean and fit and even in play fully awake, no superfluous weight or unnecessary action

quantum sutra

against the great zero of eternity
everything is insubstantial

this is what we have:
this cloud, the sea's breathing,
the dance of particle and wave
that finds us, makes us, dissolves us, and

this moment

going into the meadow after the retreat

in the meditation hall
we interrogate the silence
for a way of being human

then later again
barefoot and slow on wet spring
grass in the wild dervish storm

and back
picking twigs, ash, feathers
out of the 'no inside no outside' teachings

later, home
the horse's light breath on my cheek
the way he delicately politely

only just
meeting my eyes reads my face
hands hair with his gentle muzzle

as if he smells
questions, as if I were an event
blown in on the whirling wind

as if
from within the zero
of Zen in which he dwells

he barely
recognises me, each thing wholly
new, every encounter the first

the sound of my feet walking

walking through this huge dharma hall, the world—interrogating
(though who's asking who is a harder question) and my teachers
are the usual posse: sickness suffering old age and death

also the ruined badger the river and the uncomplaining trees,
also this web of rain taken up nest in my hair, also the dogs with
their attitude of joy

I go round the place pitying myself for my complicated life but
there's no need to seek safety or protection from all there is, no
escape either in crying or hiding not even dying

for this is the only place to be—*here* in the thick of it, and the life
of complete simplicity I say that I want will, as Eliot says, cost
me all that I have and more

'This Simone Weil called prayer'
(for Jane Hirshfield)

the way the dogs swim at twilight in the creek's high tide, and are now utterly, steadily, asleep; doing everything 'entirely and with their whole attention'

the way the *rosa rugosa* in its glass on the table almost sings; opens its petals fully, its scent filling the room like a bell whose sound keeps on coming

the way I come back from retreat knowing that so small a thing as being here is big enough to hold the whole world

Fishing boat

In the tidespill boats rock, masts tuned to the gale, playing it like blind Ossian's harp. This is the art I would like to perfect: to be a vessel for light and cloudplay, being only oneself without knowledge of oneself, in flux, at the nexus of ocean and sky and riding that dance in stillness, yielding, fluid, tethered only to each moment and every passing wave beneath the keel. To know nothing of fear, or striving.

Open the gate, unlock it, unscrew the hasp, kick it in—whatever it takes to break the ego's deadlock, let the self run free into the long grass of everything. Slip through the crack between this world and the other

naked.

Kneel; scoop silence like a benison from the aquifer beneath your feet.

Tonight, under this shifting coloured sky, everything then falls away. You are walking, walking, staff of quickbeam, oiled boots—the long view, the green note that calls you away over these hills, where you will be another indigo handprint on the hem of night.

Fletcherscombe

Walking these lanes in the green flames
of a wet high summer, meadowsweet
seeding itself and blackberries' cusp of purple,

absence of swifts, and dusk
coming on across the meadow

> it's where the light fades
> that we begin to see most clearly

a spider's thread of meaning, almost graspable
luminous as dawn, as the possibility of angels

the track nearly submerged, leading your feet away

> on the edges of vision
> the arrow lands, the stuck thing quivers

and something in you goes out, a dissolution.

The mortification of matter opens up
the heart, the Christian mystics thought—

> propitiation of dark gods
> so the new might enter in.

In the green chapel the altar-candle flickers.
The patina on leaves. A littering of light.
The possibility of flight; and then the leaving.

What-are-the-birds-doing-with-the-December-sky rap

Winter lounges, sodden and unused—
the sky is a washing-line of sorrows.

At night, the stream talks to itself;
becomes a dance floor for wintersong.

*

The wind does not care for my
predictions or predicaments;
                              like everything,
it suspires, expires, rises again.

*

Day wakes, laden with blue.

I wonder how much words weigh,
and why the oak log splitting under the axe
shows sinews haphazard as memory;

and how it is that we can hold on
to nothing, even love.

*

All truths in the end are symbolic.

I am a metaphor for transience,
just as a bird is a metaphor for flight

—how a synchronisation of starlings
is an incarnation of wind,
maybe an act of God.

*

When the ash tree fell in the woods
its bunched keys hung like a roosting
flock of pipistrelles.

In my sleep, I said: leave
access points under the eaves
for swallows, bats, angelic hosts.

You heard me. Held me close.

'January's Full Moon is called the Wolf Moon'

i
brittle cold; old fireworks lying on the gravel like spent stars that
we stumble over

and old gods looking both ways, howling over the trees that
came down in the woods last week

ii
the dog still bellying down in every rill or puddle, even in frost

iii
I remember dawns so steely we scraped plates of ice from inside
the van's windows, daughter snug between us in layers of sheep-
oiled fleece

(I remember the moon quickening in my belly, her tides and
flux; and me struck from her silver coinage)

and bare-breasted mornings working outdoors
bee-languor afternoons under the larch where you would take
me in your arms and hold me

iv
I have never told anyone *I need you*   perhaps this has been a
mistake

v
you're rolling a cigarette, your feet bare and earthy and wet
against my skin and we're waiting

in half-light the twin birds of your eyes are the only things that
move in this winter grove

to pass the time you sing; you are a male voice choir of one

and when at last we emerge into spring, Orpheus, I'll call you;
and again, Orpheus

In the time of no time

The bead curtain of the rain at the door's threshold, the way rain's contours soften the winter hills and trees. Beyond, mist snags in the teasels. Sheep bells fill the valley like a river.

Later the boar, hearing us, fled. I thought it was the windrush in the canopy of last year's leaves. Caught the last glimpse of their hurtle through the oakwood, five of them, hairy, snorting.

You walk ahead; you are essentially solitary, a mountain man.

The cairn I make for you, on this your birthday, balanced on the ridge at the end of the ride, limen between here and there, now and then, may last, may fall. You ask me what it means. I can't say. To mark a place and a moment, maybe. A gift, an offering, a celebration, small precarious monument to precarious early—

An orientation?

To see the path, you need first to squint through the hole in the top stone, close-up, then step back and let it rise towards first your eyes and then your feet.

On the limestone brow
los tres peyres in low sun
dance their slow stone dance.

The cycles of it all. We move between speech and silence, between intimacy and the less permeable space we each inhabit, on our own. Later I will think of the cairn, its stillness, how it consists of moss and stone grown so close they've become integral, yet each retains its own essential nature.

Your hands are in my hair. Sunset lights up the far hill for a brief instant.

We begin the walk
back down in bosky gloaming
towards the future.

How can I speak of silence?

The wind, the flames' roar, the greenfinch in the honeysuckle; the tone of the bell. The world, breathing—

> this stormy day
> against the window
> the tulips'
>   shout

In the night, the wind strips all the leaves. Our precision of language, our need to possess, both dissolve. I am neither here nor not here, but your here-ness, the nearness of your heartbeat—this matters.

By the river, the lilac is still dewy. I'm so immersed in its scent that I take the wrong path. The river's furrowed; overflows into my chest. The gravity of water; the weight of air. Yielding to nothing.

> This moment—
> against the torrent of eternity
>
>   breakfast

and croissants. The coffee's strong, hot, and we refill the pot speaking of the mysteries
>   and so

> breakfast overflows
> into zazen
> into everything

Five people have boiled eggs. I fry mine so that I can use the perfect brown shell, the cosmic egg now cracked, as a centrepiece for silence, with lilac and bowl

this broken eggshell—
no chick, just
the great *I am* of nothing

which keeps on singing into the silence long after we've started
talking.

Feet

An inexplicable footprint on the misted glass, the five toes vulnerable in their see-through ephemeral strangely-vertical walking into darkness.

The heel of the year. This morning a wren whirred out of the shed's black nadir; and in the snow the robin's feet trace capillaries where filaments of darkness wire the yard.

Slow snow. Whiting. World hushed to only the soft tick of flake and slush of feet.

This morning the badger, dead a month now and freeze-dried, had been gutted in the night from behind, and a dark spill of organs and coiled blistering pipework jostled the ribs. She is a young female, her pads plump as any dog's, pushing against nothing.

The dead badger's paws turned towards me.

In this room there are twenty feet. Thousands of miles have been swallowed by these soles. Sorrow they've walked, and joy; the ecstasy of dance, stretching and splaying; the desire of sand on skin, the tickle of turf and trefoil; the flex and curl of sex mapped in the toes' reflex; the touch of tenderness foot to foot, straining towards the lover in the slide towards night.

Yesterday my lover's cleated bootprints put down roots in the mud of my car mat. Feet are more intimate than hands; private.

In the Lot, the shock and poignancy of that prehistoric print, 16,000 years the mother and toddler step side by side, forever walking the songlines.

        Plugged into the earth like this we walk
towards the darkness willingly,

and willing the sun to keep rising
        rising
                keep feathering your arrows of direction
                                                Helios
keep lighting the way

before the six-foot-under, the cold, which is under, right now,
my warm-booted feet.

The blood of others

Since we're spinning at seventeen miles per second and accelerating outwards towards nothing—or maybe everything—don't our molecules stream out towards the past, and isn't going back the way we know always so much swifter than travelling on?

> *Here the blackberries ripen in waves. Something the colour of memory taps at my window at night; almost I can see the birthplace of stars*

> *till daylight covers the bones with dust; and each time the beginning is just a beginning-again of something I still can't name.*

Today I read about gannets: the single egg they can't, for fear of gull reprisal, leave; and how the fledglings at three months fly from here to southern Africa; and of the millions that never make it. Those blue eyes.

> *Something is pushing from behind her eyes to get out. I read it, the whole beautiful illuminating of it, but not in words*

> *any more than I have a lexicon for the boy inert in the car park. I weep for the young soles of his feet because I cannot weep for the rest of him.*

Wind's in the northeast now, autumn in its skirts. The blood of others is always on my hands. What the wind carries: fly where you want—Antarctica, Ireland, Brazil. Your own history will still be waiting when you get back.

exclusion zone

so that they can sleep they would prefer to think that it's a dream
but it's not a dream

so that they can eat and stroll around in their freedom
they prefer not to hear

but what I want to tell you is this: there was a shoe one side
of the line, and the limb

quite the other in the exclusion zone where
silence rolled in

in a great standing wave that stopped our hearts long enough
to hear its roar

we saw one bird fly into a sky whose colour has no name
they say its wings

were burning

I want to tell you this, that the scattered grain
was red under that sky

For the Fallen 1
(after Carolyn Forché)

An arrow, tipped
An antelope poised to drink
An arsenal cached in soil and rust under the hedge
An acre of smoke on white air
An aria for the dead, their small mouths lipping the river's skin

A boy, running
A barren mare, bony and forgotten
A blue burst of mist, or gunfire
A basinful of blood, poured at dawn
A bone, nesting in another bone

A car wired to kill
A clutch of abandoned eggs
A cathedral unroofed for the rain to dance in
A cantata for the ruined city
A corpse by the roadside, uncovered

A day without sun
A day with no leaf-fall or birdsong
A day with no human voice
A day with no cessation of bullets
A day with no clothes on, a day with its eyes wide open, a day
with no owner

An earth perfectly pitched, calibrated and tilted for life
An error that costs more than the earth (an earth perfectly
poisoned, an earth that can't breathe, an earth that cannot sustain
our weight)
An entire population missing
An exclusion zone round the earth
An elegy

Maristow

i
if we could see each day
as one of the unpronounceable
names of God
if we could be breathed by it

ii
from somewhere in the reaches
of the singing spheres
light drops
enters
and fills us
spilling until we remember

the soul needs beaches

iii
angels on the pin's head

or maybe a mathematical equation
so subtle it would not tip
a balance used to weigh
the down on the quill
of a breast feather

iv
the gathering point of the bridge
the way it takes wing
across nothing

air green with wild garlic
each starry head a burst
of vowels

v
across the mudflats
curlews have not forgotten
notes a pouring of blue
into paler air

I am behind myself

then your fingertips—
a flight of words
I almost know

vi
the path unwinds between oaks
and creek

in the bank's verdant shade
for the first time the little well
is brimful and clear

water I think one
of the unpronounceable names

vii
the woods, this me, this you

now is beskiness, salty, inward
all *coniunctio*

pores tasting Other, each

the ebb-tide taking only what can be
spoken of or numbered—

the rest
irreducible

Lydford Gorge
(for Anne Jackson)

i
coinage of ash leaf,
hazel, oak—lilting
to the pool's clear breath

lichened beech twigs
like an accumulation
of small acts of kindness

ii
my friend says:
you go for months
without an epiphany
then six come along
at once

iii
the cuckoo calls twice
and is silent

iv
this white lady
pours her whole self
the dragon of her
hair
like white fire
through the forest gorge

long after we leave
her dark moist places
her thunder
roars through my cells

v
Greta said last night
the connection between mime
and poetry
might be silence

vi
this might be true too
of love—I mean that silence
is the lodestone

vii
he writes to me
of the wood
the cabin he's built
the green air

he speaks of
my absence

viii
I want a dress
like moonshine and water

I want to slip through the crack
between this world
and the other
naked

ix
you can never step in the same
river twice, say the teachings

x
all my rivers
are inside

Summer Solstice, Merrivale

[After the horrors of battle] a strange madness came upon Myrddin . . . Into the forest he went, glad to lie hidden beneath the ash trees. He watched the wild creatures grazing on the pastures of the glades. He made use of the roots of plants and of grasses, of fruit from trees and of the blackberries in the thicket. He became a Man of the Woods, Myrddin Wyllt, as if dedicated to the woods. So for a whole summer he stayed hidden in the woods, discovered by none, forgetful of himself and of his own, lurking like a wild thing.

      (*Vita Merlini*, Geoffrey of Monmouth, ca. 1150)

i
in the ruins of the old school house
(four winds, one beech tree
two ragged skewbalds)

nine writers
open the notebook of day

ii
red-sheathed bog cotton
flutters its pennants like snags of cloud
misplaced thoughts
or prayer-flags

iii
lift this granite pebble
from the ochre stream bed
from the water's conversations

the pebble's granite angles
receive and transmit light
resist my palm

iv
the year has come to fruition
what still needs release
before the slide through harvest-time
back to the fallows?

v
after the battles and bloodshed
what remains is peace

the mysteries of love
are stronger than the mysteries
of death

vi
we walk the pairs of stones
in our procession
in a covenant with the past
and with silence

vii
in the 11 stones of the circle
its 4000-year-long discourse
with leaf bird stone wind sky
the day is both clear and opaque

vii
the winds skim our heads
but we've stilled
condensed to light and shadow

we put on the woods of the drovers' track
like a green cloak

viii
Su says
I wear my dad on the inside, his heart
the land listens

ix
the pebble is a passing moment
stalled into matter and time
stony bones reassembled
like mine
from atoms
dust of fallen stars

and all of us
spinning in space

x
the pebble is
my contract
with silence

xi
in the world's hurry
this will endure

Entering the wood

Where

the periphery path
               is a flattened hemisphere
       in fact it's
half a heart

*

entering the green eye of the woods
    you go naked
as in the presence of a lover
    or a god
stripped of the might-have-been selves
       and all that is not now
               or here

crossing the threshold with the whole of you
    and all that fecund body stretched out above, around,
                 below you

*

the old gods linger still
    where the trees have eyes
and twigs finger your passing

       stories in the soil and the palimpsest of history
which is here, now, as we are, flickering, present—not vertical,
               of time,
    but horizontal, stitched into the green spaces and
             throbbing around us—

in the language of wodwose and dryad
flower maiden and green man

and the green lady kneels with her earth-dark hands
                and the wood is a living and fertile presence

there are voices here

*

the moist darkness
the bursting soil
     its unthinkable numbers of lives
their separate rhythms pulsing
                     as one

*

winter solstice
tides of tattered leaves
    husks of nuts, squirrel-gnawed

tales of dead wood and winter

blowing on our fingers
    whorls of breath curling the blue air

burning the old year
        our worn-out hopes and fears with it

again the tidying
        trimming dead wood

the burial of tattyrags

all over there are bonfires—
                beacons against the coming of the dark

*

February is coppicing
    spring-cleaning the wood

        remembering line, vaulting, architecture
    thinning hazel scrub
      to let in summer
when it comes

    the pattern of our saws
their dissonant harmonies
      weak sun on our backs
thin feather of smoke
    and the showers of rufous catkins
  around our feet
      the mallet's knock
its echo

        on the road the erratic pulse
    of traffic
    we think of tidying our lives

*

and so it begins again with
    a thickening of the light
strong spikes of bluebells
           pushing towards air

wild garlic
    the smell of it beneath our boots brimming
first snowdrops, violets, custard splash of primrose
    sorrel leaves
        anemone leaf-tendrils

             the scrabbling woodmouse
          whiskers twitching
eyes meeting yours for a flash and then gone

             yaffle of woodpecker

and soon the swallows' return

          time of fly orchids and campion

             planted

all our fertile yearnings
          bare in the greening of the year

light spills
             the year begins
          in the open mouth
                              of spring

*

The wheel of the year
          turns through its spheres and seasons
the spikes of growth, the cycles of decay

             shallow times
          and deeper times
             fallow times
          and full—

and here's the rub: creatures
of night and day both

we mislay ourselves somewhere
        maybe forever
in the siren strait between the two

all seems lost

*

                and then
                all is not lost
                but waiting to return

*

when the fire has gone
and the wood, and the day itself
what linger are our hands

*

*The wheel turns
in the darkness*

                *the heart cracks open
                this green blood
                these few words*

This is our time

Heavy rains
                the heart hurting for water
                                its lonely hunt

At the summit of the bony hill
                this one brief bloom

and a long life's longing
                        for itself.

*

All summer drought
                and now the deluge

                        no arks—

        and no covenants either.

*

There are times when the only answer is silence.

Months then when the dance may last
                                all month.

The moon rises, fattens and falls.

                        Our work of bringing back
        the soul
                looks for and fails to find
steadiness.

The tabernacle remains unvisited.

*

Even if you don't believe in God
                    rhythms and patterns prevail
and recreate themselves.

Where you find yourself
            is a land as vast and unknown

as the seabed

a hard ticking in the blood
                    of lush
                                uncertainty

that ripe territory
            between presence and absence.

Promise
            and the crops it delivers
                    or reabsorbs.

This morning
            a glut of light
                    a slender world.

*

These bodies we wear—agglomerations
            of earth and sunlight

bones blood flesh nerves sinews cells
desires hopes fears

longings.

How grateful I am today
        for those who
give themselves to this
                over and over—

listening for one true word.

*

Frontiers change.

Not a leaf moves; not a bird calls.
        I don't know how long
we stare at each other.
        We don't know how long we have.

Only the moment counts.

There is a drumbeat passes
from cell to cell
        a hot wind hopscotching
                over the synapses.

Listen—somewhere there is a question
                knocking   and knocking.

Silence your heart
     and listen
     with all of yourself.

*

That nomansland.

Winds and moors that drive you to madness

    and love

       which is always a form of madness.

We all need something to stand between us and the horizon
    to snag that white butterfly of the passing moment
as it slips past gauzy
      on its way back
    to where it came from. Between us and
the horror of eternity.

I need you. There: I say
    the unsayable.

I need you.

Call down the fat-bellied moon

    remember.

*

There are cycles of blood and bone.

       Times when the harvest fails
and then suddenly more than you can feast on, the golden
ground
       engorged with fallen fruit.

They've baled the straw now
       shorn the fields.

*

             Bring on the sacrificial one

       I am
Corn Maiden, May Queen and Crone.
You the Green Man, Cernunnos, Herne and the deer he runs
with
         and the one who runs him down

Three days in the dark
       or hung from the tree

and over and over
         the quarantine.

We are the hunter and the hunted
       saved and damned.

In the July dusk
        our mouths are red
                with berries.

*

Was it Eliot who said
        A thing is most fully itself
        when here and now cease to matter?

*

Over the rising tide

                the moon
                    rises

                              again.

Your fingers play my spine.

*

She said:
        He needs you to be lodestone and lodestar
        he needs you to be true.

Times when we're both compass and north, depthsounder
                          and ocean.

*

Now the tide floods the road
       and summer's thirst is slaked
You wear snakes like bracelets

and in my dreams
      the flaming arrows ignite the heavens
            like bright unearthly fireworks.

We are falling stars

The wind passes by, a siffle
      in the canopy.

*

Let me be steady
      as that beech vibrating in her
          still silent dance
in that holy grove.

This is our time.

*

We shall build this day that's a boat
    of larch
       of oak
          of riverlight

care will be the rivets

her beam will be broad
     we'll sit deep in the rolling waves.

The floods will not drown her.

See how the bow ploughs clean
     and she skims the water
               like a fulmar

and see how her nose unfailingly
is set on course for home.

Undercliff sutra

i
and so it goes on

in wet grass stalking
a poem amid notions
of no-self
and not knowing
except in small moments
like this, where for an instant
the path becomes smooth
allows a glimpse

ii
or there, low tide
two seals in the shallows
our bare feet
gleaming in nacreous
dusk
and only sky and ocean
(undifferentiated)
and this is all there is

iii
even a path that leads beyond
the illusions of things
is still a path of belief

today I believe in the colour of leaves
in the sturdy growth on the undercliff
in the fingertips of drizzle

iv
there
I was naked
even when fully clothed

I have been crowned with stars
I have been a snake
in the grass too

honesty as elusive
as unconditional love
or fireflies

v
we arrive at the harbour
and it's the same boat we choose always
eye of Horus farseeing
on the prow, chipped paintwork—
even though she hasn't been caulked
even though the engine misfires
even though the sails are tatty

still she takes us to where
we need to be

vi
I have not always been honest
though I talk about honesty

a être deshonnête ce n'est pas seulement
à dire ce qui n'est pas vrai
mais c'est aussi à ne pas dire ce qui est vrai

on the cliffs the air twitches
half-light
half-dark

vii
easy to ask
'how did I end up here?'

harder and more real is
'what did I not get wrong?'

and ah the trust, the risk
the leaps of faith

to let the ocean take you
and the soul

viii
the centre is always at hand
even when out of reach

leaves flicker
morning will come
still we walk forward
maybe begin to

dance

*The French quote is a paraphrase
of a line by Albert Camus.*

'One word like a sun'
(Octavio Paz)

chewing away at syntax
until the
word
the world
comes loose

and floats

wolf at
the door gnawing
her own paw

the sound of

one word
punctuation of
griefpainjoysadnessfearlovehate
truth

bird
one bird flapping

time
oh yes this huge this dharma hall
the world

the question
how
a bigger question
why

coming free coming
out coming on
coming along

coming through
coming by coming
home

the rain
shakes
the tree
shakes the sun loose
shakes one word

THIS

being here

rain in leaves, thin sun sprinkling
the wrinkled winter creek
where wild geese fly

being here sheltered in the lamp's
glow, imagining for a moment
that these faces have only ever

known light

Atoms

it's not the words that count
it's what flickers in the
quickening ground
between them

listen: what calls you back
over and over, insists on that
single syllable, home, home, home?

last night, moon on the hill
how many times before
have I been leaf, bird,
single blade of grass?

copper beech shakes itself all over the thin roof

waiting for something
to kickstart my heart

standing in the river
the mind a leaky bucket
missing the point

spell for the spirit of fire

once I was greenwood
I died, and rose from the dead—
now I speak in tongues of red

The white noise of the universe

The stars are in our belly; the Milky Way
our umbilicus. Is it a consolation
that the stuff of which we're made is star-stuff too?

Wherever you go you can never totally disappear—
dispersal only: carbon, hydrogen, nitrogen, oxygen.
Tree, rain, coal, glow-worm, horse, gnat, rock.

If you tune everything else out
the silence you hear is the white noise
of the singing spheres: the voice of the universe.

Now, dusk; all the available light—
yellow, cyan, magenta—
inhaled and re-emitted by cranesbill, loosestrife, muskmallow.

My hand, making these words.